Principles
of Ministry
& Faith

Principles

of Ministry
& Faith

Applying godly principles to your life and ministry.

RICH LAMMAY

XULON PRESS

Xulon Press
2301 Lucien Way #415
Maitland, FL 32751
407.339.4217
www.xulonpress.com

Printed in the United States of America.

ISBN-13: 978-1-6628-0746-6

DEDICATION

All thanks go to God who in 1975 took an ignorant and foolish young man and called him to be His son and has allowed him to serve Him all these years.

A special thank you to the men who have so influenced my life and ministry.

Pastor Dawson Wheeler
Pastor Skip Collier
Pastor Jon Courson
Gayle D. Erwin
Pastor Leo Kruger (my friend)

And mostly to my godly wife, (Suzanne) whom the Lord has graciously given me as my patient and loving life partner.

CONTENTS

INTRODUCTION

W hen I set out to write this book, my original idea was to document the Principles of Ministry I have been able to learn over the many years I've been serving Christ. Then, as I began writing, I quickly realized the Principles of Ministry, which God had laid on my heart; apply in one degree or another to every Christian. So, my writing turned into a bit of a mixture of Principles of Ministry and Principles of Faith.

Of course, none of these principles are unique to me or to any Pastor. Many godly men and women have laid a foundation for others to follow and I have seen these principles at work in many believers from different church backgrounds and denominations, all of whom example "servant leadership". Most of the principles found in this book I have gleaned from some of the wonderful mentors God has placed in my life; including but not limited to: Gayle D. Erwin, Pastor Jon Courson and Dr. Larry Taylor and his insightful booklet; "Things I learned from my Pastor". I thank God for these men and many others who have planted within me the principles which lead to a solid and Biblical ministry and a consistent walk with the Lord.

Still, my personal experience as a pastor of almost thirty years, has shown me when ministries or individuals function according to these principles they will be blessed and will grow spiritually. Those with a different view of serving Christ are often the ones who live in chaos and are not fulfilling the Great Commission.

The principles in this book are not in a particular order nor should they be looked at as an exhaustive list of things to do in order to be Spirit filled. While these principles should be considered foundational to every Pastor and church leader, they also apply, to one degree or another to every Jesus follower because these Principles of Ministry and Faith are principles for godly living.

As you read each principle, if you are involved in ministry filter them through the lens of your personal life as well as the calling God has for you. If you are not involved in ministry, use the overall principle to examine your own faith walk as well as a benchmark for the church you attend.

When these principles are foundational to any of God's people from Pastors to laypeople, they will bear much fruit for the Lord. And that's exactly what God's people are called to do, to bear good fruit for Jesus.

> **John 15:16 (Jesus said) "You did not choose me, but I chose you and appointed you to go and bear fruit — fruit that will last..."**

Bearing good fruit unto the Lord is not only the calling of every Jesus follower, it's where there is fullness of joy.

because as you bear good fruit, you are in the very will of God. So, let me leave this introduction with a challenge for all of us.

CHALLENGE: Read the Principles of Ministry and Faith with a heart open to what God wants to do in both your personal life and any ministry you may be involved with.

Chapter One

BE SPIRIT LED

Zechariah 4:6 "...Not by might nor by power, but by My Spirit, says the Lord of hosts."

E very Christian is in the ministry because Jesus called all his followers to be both salt and light to the world. Because we're all called to ministry, every Christian must rely on the supernatural power of the Holy Spirit in order to serve the Lord.

Church leadership and those involved in frontline ministry must be Spirit led all the more because they are setting the example for the rest of the body and are guarding them from the fiery darts of the enemy. Personally, I have found times in my life when I've walked in the Spirit and other times when I was walking in the flesh more than the Spirit. It's the times when I'm in tune with the Holy Spirit that ministry flows and good fruit is evident.

When a church is not Spirit led, they'll turn to philosophies and programs to do God's work but the church belongs to God and Jesus said, *"I will build my church!"*

It's His work therefore the church, just like the individual Christian, must be led by the Holy Spirit in everything.

As Henry Blackaby said in his book "Experiencing God"; "We don't choose what we will do for God; He invites us to join Him where He wants to involve us." In other words; Find out where the Holy Spirit is working and join in what He is doing. To do so, you must seek His will, confess your personal inabilities and rest on His strength. How easy it is to fall into the trap of relying on self, especially in areas where you're naturally gifted.

Sadly, much of the western church today is filled with programs that promote, "how to do ministry". There are seminars and conferences showing how to raise money, attract new members, administrate, counsel, or evangelize. While you may glean some good concepts from these programs, one main key to successful ministry is not to rely on a technique, book or seminar instead you must seek the guidance of the Holy Spirit. Look to Him in prayer and search God's Word because that's where you'll find direction for ministry and for your life.

> *2 Peter 1:3 "His divine power has given us everything we need for life and godliness through our knowledge of him who called us by his own glory and goodness."*

I love that verse, because it reminds me that whatever I need for godliness comes from knowing Jesus better and it is by prayer and from God's word that I will discover all

I need. So, it's the Holy Spirit who gives inspiration and shows you what God wants. The Spirit will also instill vision for where God is guiding you personally as well as what He wants in the ministry entrusted to you.

Today many church programs are adopted directly from the world. Some evangelism programs are based on worldly sales techniques such as "branding your ministry". Administrative courses are often based on business management principles, which can be helpful but prayer should guide the church. Some counseling techniques come from secular psychology and the "science of church growth" is often based on demographics and marketing strategies. Of course, those things might work in the sense you can build an organization with those tactics but the problem is; it may not be what the Lord wants in His church. As Dr. Larry Taylor says (in his booklet "Things I learned from my pastor") "If you build it with the world's techniques, you will have to maintain it with those same methods."

Setting aside the "how to instructions" can be hard but in the long run it's easier than striving to build God's work with worldly approaches. When you let God do His work, it takes the worry out of ministry because it's His work and that's when you can relax and join with what God is doing. Your responsibility is to seek His will, rely on His Spirit, and obey Him. That means, if God has guided you in an area, He will provide whatever you need and will help you address any problems that arise.

As you rely on God, God should get the glory and it's vital that God gets the credit for what He does, and you take the blame for what you do. Again Dr. Taylor says it well; "Just as God will not share His glory with any person so He should not share the credit for your failures." All the credit and praise must go to Christ because He's the head of His church and if He's building it the church belongs to Him. But if you're building it you have to ask; who does the church belong to?

It's vital that God gets the credit for what He does, and you take the blame for what you do.

Being Spirit led must apply to the individual as well. Every Christian should ask themselves; "Am I building my life on the guidance of the Spirit? Or am I being directed by the flesh?" What about your family? What about your personal devotions? Are you trying to complete in the flesh what was begun in the Spirit? *(Galatians 3:3)*

Being led by the Spirit is not always easy but it does bring peace. The Spirit is called; "the Spirit of peace", so you'll find peace as you rely on the Spirit. Peace comes because when you're in the will of God because peace is the Holy Spirit's fruit. And peace comes as you see God provide whatever is needed for what He's called you to do.

Over the years people have suggested different ideas for ministry and persuaded me to adopt a program or start a particular ministry. Sometimes those ideas have worked out but more often than not they bore little fruit. I have learned if someone has a ministry idea, first find out if they're qualified and willing to lead it. If they are, it just might be the Holy Spirit, and if not, I've learned to pray and wait on God.

As I pray, I believe God will show me what to do or not to do, or He will provide what is needed for the situation.

How will God provide? It may be materially or it may in a person who has the calling to that new ministry. Or maybe God will give me the vision to see what he wants to do. No matter how God guides, when you follow the Spirit you can know God will give you the good things you need.

> *(Jesus said) "If you then, who are evil, know how to give good gifts to your children, how much more will the heavenly Father give the Holy Spirit to those who ask him!" Luke 11:13 ESV*

God wants to give you the Holy Spirit and all you need do is ask. The Spirit's work starts with the conviction of the unbeliever then continues as He guides the believer into all truth. Still, too many in the church think the gifting of the Spirit is something that's limited to a meeting where they hear a message from God but nothing ever changes in their life.

While the working of the Spirit (especially in the gifts of the Spirit) is exciting, it's not always proof God is working. People are often moved by emotions or sadly some will use what they say is the moving of the Spirit to manipulate others. The gifts of the Spirit exist to build up the believers and equip the church for the work God has given. *(Ephesians 2:10)* When the Spirit is moving in a church service or in the individual's life, the result should always be good fruit, and the building up of the body of Christ. *(Galatians 5:22-23)*

> *1 Corinthians 14:12 says; "...Since you are eager to have spiritual gifts, try to excel in gifts that build up the church."*

It's good to desire the gifts of the Spirit, but every believer should want to be used in the gifts that edify rather than gifts which divide. Sadly, too often division is exactly what happens because people are more focused on the gift instead of being focused on the Gift Giver. The church can become divided by those who have (what they deem) "greater gifts" pitting them against those who have "lesser" gifts.

The truly Spirit led person is Spirit led in all they do and that means they are ready for whatever the Spirit has for them. They're always looking for where He's working, and making sure God gets the glory for what he does. Being Spirit led means you get to participate in the work and the will of God and there's no more exciting place than the will of God.

Charles Spurgeon said; "A church in the land without the Spirit is rather a curse than a blessing. If you have not the Spirit of God, Christian worker, remember that you stand in somebody else's way; you are a fruitless tree standing where a fruitful tree might grow."

The only way to be truly fruitful is to be led by the Spirit in all you do. How does that work, you ask? I have found that I hear the Spirit better when three things are working in

6

my life; First, I'm in the Word of God on a consistent basis. Secondly, I'm praying each day for my needs and about the burdens on my heart. And finally, I'm serving others.

With the Word of God speaking and prayer guiding and while I'm following Jesus example of serving, that's when the Holy Spirit speaks the loudest.

CHALLENGE: Wait on the Holy Spirit to guide you before jumping into ministry but follow the Holy Spirit in what he's already said in His Word. Consider what God's word says about your position of life and ask yourself; "Am I living out what God already has revealed for me as (a husband, wife, single, Sunday school teacher...) fill in the blank.

Chapter Two

BE A SERVANT

Matthew 23:11-12 "The greatest among you will be your servant. For whoever exalts himself will be humbled, and whoever humbles himself will be exalted." (Matthew 18:1-4, Mark 9; Luke 9&22)

It's been said that the way up in God's kingdom is to work your way to the bottom. More than once Jesus had to teach his disciples about servanthood. He taught; if you are going to be used by God, you must learn to serve others because the Lord's way is the exact opposite of the world's way.

For many years I worked in the corporate world where I was exposed to different leadership styles. Some leaders were autocratic while others were charismatic but the most successful leaders were those who served those under their leadership. Servanthood is Jesus style of leadership and servanthood must be the way God's people lead. It doesn't matter if you have a position in the church or in your home; the way of the Lord is always opposed to the ways of the world.

If the church has a flow chart it would look like an inverted pyramid because in God's economy the least becomes the greatest and the servant of all. Os Guinness once said; "Jesus made clear that the Kingdom of God is organic and not organizational. It grows like a seed and it works like leaven: secretly, invisibly, surprisingly, and irresistibly." While there may be nothing wrong with an organizational chart as such, the idea that the one at the top has the most privilege is counter to Jesus model for ministry.

Every church leader must understand; the higher up you go in the church it means you have more opportunities to serve. Our example is Jesus, who although He was God Incarnate, He put on a towel, knelt down, and did the work of a servant by washing stinky feet. *(John 13)*

Today, many in the church and way too many in frontline ministry act as if they're greater than Jesus. Remember, the word "ministry" means service! It means serving others inside and outside the church. Jesus said; even giving a cup of cool water will be rewarded, so in ministry you see what needs done and you do it. That means you consider no task beneath you and no task above you. If something needs to be done,

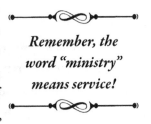

Remember, the word "ministry" means service!

"just do it!" If there's trash, pick it up, if a light is out, change it, if the nursery is short of help – maybe you should jump in a do what needs to be done.

On the flip side, if God calls you to something and you feel as if you're not qualified to do, remember that's His problem and know; if God called you to it, He'll equip you to do what He has led you to do.

Before you can apply those principles to the church you must first apply them to your home. The believing husband is to love his wife just like Christ loved the church. The wife is called to submit to the authority God has given her husband and both husband and wife are to respect one another and submit to one another out of reverence for Christ *(Ephesians 5:21)*. All the church is to serve one another and carry one another's burdens because that's a command and that's how we fulfill the law of Christ *(Galatians 6:2)*.

Some people want to be used by God but they never serve others, other people might be willing to help but they have to be told what to do. But a true minister of the Gospel is one who serves God's people and they are aware of what needs done, so, they do it. A true servant is the one who straightens out the chairs after study, picks up trash after the service or helps the needy to their car. That's how church leaders should be and that's how the church can recognize future leaders. A true leader has a heart for people and they serve God by serving others. And a true servant of Christ understands that servanthood begins in the home. They know that love in action is the mark of a true Jesus follower.

Jesus said; *"The harvest is plentiful, but the workers are few." (Luke 10:2)* There are many who want a title or position, but servants are rare. That's why Jesus said to pray for more workers. Motivated by love for God and God's people, a servant leader serves and blesses God's people.

One important principle in serving is; those you serve should be able to relate to you. I believe those in fulltime ministry should live a simple lifestyle in order to relate to God's people. If your standard of living is far above the people you're serving, you will no longer be seen as a servant. In recent years we have seen way too many church leaders fall because of greed and a lust for power. They have lost their reputation and their ministry because they forgot what Paul warned Timothy.

> *1 Timothy 6:10 For the love of money is a root of all kinds of evils. It is through this craving that some have wandered away from the faith and pierced themselves with many pangs. ESV*

Although the worker is worth of his wages; those wages should not be out of line with what most of the church's members make. A servant leader should always be willing to take a job outside the ministry (as said about Paul, "make tents") when needed. Sadly, many involved in ministry will leave and look for another situation if the church's finances get too low.

> *Matthew 20:25-28 "You know that the rulers of the Gentiles lord it over them, and their high officials exercise authority over them. Not so with you. Instead, whoever wants to become great*

among you must be your servant, and whoever wants to be first must be your slave— just as the Son of Man did not come to be served, but to serve, and to give his life as a ransom for many."

Because you love God's people, you serve them and the first way you serve is by being an example to them. You're an example by helping, assisting, and blessing others, because that's your calling. If you're really called to ministry, you'll never outgrow service. It's not something to do until the church is big enough because serving Christ is always about serving others. Never forget Jesus words;

Matthew 23:11 "The greatest among you shall be your servant." ESV

I think it's important to remember that ministry is a verb. In other words, ministry involves action. Jesus said in *John 13:15 "I have set you an example that you should do as I have done for you."* If you want to follow the example of Jesus you serve those God has in your life. If you're a servant of God you'll minister to those God puts in your life and not try to get them to minister to you. Sadly, many in ministry seem to want to be served and want people to minister to them, rather than blessing others. You see this attitude when someone strives for more authority or tries to get money from people.

It could be the televangelist who's always begging for money or the pastor who accuses the church of not taking care of him. It might be a subtle manipulation to get people to praise and encourage you or sadly, outright manipulation is not uncommon in the church. Be that as it may, as Christ's servant, you are not seeking anything for yourself but you're dead in Christ and those who are dead to self just believe God will take care of everything they need. God will supply your financial needs and He'll meet your emotional needs. It's your responsibility to deny self, take up your cross and follow Jesus by fufilling your calling as you care for others.

If there is a central principle of Christian ministry it was summed up by General William Booth, the founder of the Salvation Army. One time he sent a message to his co-laborers which contained only one word: "Others". And "Others" was the focus of both his life and ministry. Even to this day the Salvation Army meets the practical needs of millions of people around the world.

Those in ministry should live for others and not self. Church leadership should seek to bless, not to be blessed; to love, not to be loved; to care for and not to be cared for; and to minister to others and not be ministered to.

For those in pastoral ministry; you're called to feed God's people with God's Word and to serve them in love. The title Pastor means Shepherd, so a Pastor should live for God's people and care for God's church because that's what real Shepherds do.

If you're in the ministry to get your own needs met, either repent, or quit! Jesus is looking for people with a heart for God's church. Like when Jesus wept over Jerusalem,

He still desires to gather His children as a hen protects her chicks. If you're involved in ministry, your calling is to bring God's people into the loving arms of Jesus because He is our loving, good Shepherd.

If you are not in an official ministry you're still called to serve in love. Every believer, even those without a title or position, must demonstrate love for one another showing themselves to be Jesus followers *(John 13:35)*. You're called to love and to demonstrate love, because love, just like ministry is a verb.

I think it's important to see how the great love chapter of the Bible describes love in the terms of actions and behaviors. The Apostle Paul described love in action terms because that's how God showed his love to us and that's how we show the world God's great love.

> *1 Corinthians 13:4-8 Love is patient and kind; love does not envy or boast; it is not arrogant or rude. It does not insist on its own way; it is not irritable or resentful; it does not rejoice at wrongdoing, but rejoices with the truth. Love bears all things, believes all things, hopes all things, endures all things. Love never fails"...ESV*

That text should cause every Christian to stop and evaluate their life. While each virtue of love is found in Jesus Christ, it's also where you are led as you walk in the Spirit. Remember the fruit of the Spirit (singular) is love *(Galatians 5:22)*, and love is the benchmark of being a disciple of Jesus. If we do not pass the love test, then it's time to repent and be filled with the Spirit because love is the key to being a servant and ministry is always demonstrated by actions that are motivated by love.

CHALLENGE: Examine your heart and your actions, ask yourself; "Am I a servant or do I want to be served?" And, how do you respond when someone treats you like a servant?

Then, using 1 Corinthians 13:4-8, examine your faith. It's the benchmark to see if you're living in love. Ask yourself; "Am I patient, loving and kind (etc.) to the people God has in my life?"

> *"...All who are led by the Spirit of God are children of God." (Romans 8:14 NLT).*

Chapter Three

DON'T SWEAT IT!

Philippians 2:13 *"For it is God who works in you both to will and to do for His good pleasure."*

D r. Larry Taylor says: "If you're building your own ministry, you'll find the work strenuous. But if you rely on the supernatural power of the Holy Spirit, you can trust God and ministry will flow. You might get tired in the work involved in ministry, but you should never be tired of the work of ministry. "Burn out" is unthinkable when you take your rest in Jesus."

Chuck Smith used to say; "God wants inspiration, not perspiration." Like the High Priest of Israel, as they performed their priestly duty, they were to wear linen and never wool. Why linen and not wool? Because wool makes you sweat. If you try to "pump up" a ministry by your own efforts your success will be based on your performance and perspiration. But if you rely on the Holy Spirit and His gifts, you can go with the flow and watch God work.

Today many churches rely on programs, hyped up worship or emotionalism to build the ministry. If you do that eventually you will get exhausted as you will have to work hard to maintain what you have built.

I have been in churches where emotionalism is common place. They place a huge emphasis on the moving of the Holy Spirit within the gifts they deem as most important. They must continually "police" things which become strange and out of order. Other churches try to build their ministry on "awesome worship" so they hire professional musicians who can move you with their skills. Sadly, in some of these churches very few people are singing praises to the Lord but many are watching the band perform.

Maintaining ministry built on human talent, emotionalism or even a dynamic personality will eventually become a burden to keep going. True inspiration comes from a heart yielded to God and a life continually filled with the Holy Spirit.

> *Galatians 5:16 ESV "But I say, walk by the Spirit, and you will not gratify the desires of the flesh."*

The verb "to walk" implies action on your part, and if you continue to read Galatians chapter 5 it becomes apparent that the Christian can walk in the flesh or walk in the Spirit. So, ask yourself: Which one are you walking in?

When you walk in the Spirit you will naturally take steps of faith, then stepping out, you'll see if God wants to do something through you. If it's not His will or His timing, you can let go and move on. But sometimes it is God's will and the right time, so as you take a step of faith you see good fruit because God was just waiting for someone (like Peter) to step out of the boat.

When you recognize God is in charge, and Jesus is building His church (without your help), you can relax and let go of any strife and worry. Sometimes it's obvious when God is not in a particular venture because there's a lack of fruit. That's when you have to let it go, but that's not always easy because it may have become a tradition or some people like a particular program.

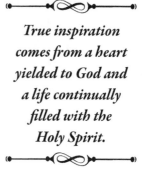

True inspiration comes from a heart yielded to God and a life continually filled with the Holy Spirit.

It's important that everyone involved in ministry must constantly be looking at ministry with fresh eyes to see where God is moving. If He's not moving in a certain place, let it go and move on. But where you see God working that's where you want to put your efforts. You want to be ministering where God is working and when you are, things will be less of a burden, there will be good fruit, and you won't have to sweat it.

A word of caution; Always put the Word of God as the priority over any "revelation". I remember when a woman in the church I was attending had a great ministry to women around the western United States; then she had a "revelation". What was her revelation? She was to leave her husband and children and go "full time" for Jesus. Sorry, that's placing feelings before God's word. The revealed Word of God, through the Canon of Scripture, is preeminent over any feelings or revelation. If something is contrary to what God has already revealed to us, it's not from the Holy Spirit, and that's an absolute because God will never contradict His Word.

There's no sweat in ministry and no turmoil in life when you realize your life is to give glory to God and how you do that is found within the pages of your Bible.

CHALLENGE: Look through fresh eyes at your life and ministry. Are you striving to keep something going that has no fruit? Are you living out what God has already revealed in his word? Are you preempting God's word by not trusting what he has for you?

Chapter Four

BE FLEXIBLE

Acts 8:26 "Now an angel of the Lord said to Philip,
"Go south to the road — the desert road — that
goes down from Jerusalem to Gaza."

It's been said; "Blessed are the flexible, they shall not be broken!" Philip was in Samaria where there was a great movement of God, but God wanted him to go to the desert because there was someone Philip needed to speak to. In the natural it seemed foolish to leave a revival and go to the unknown, but Philip went and brought the Ethiopian Eunuch to faith who in turn took the Gospel with him.

The principle of flexibility is a necessity if you're following the Spirit because you can't follow the Spirit without being flexible. Lack of flexibility is why some churches like the pre-packaged programs or canned sermons. It's easier to follow a program because you know what to do and when to do it, and it can drive the flesh crazy not to have everything planned out.

True ministry must be flexible and ready to be used by God at any time and in whatever way He wants. If you're not flexible, you will break. I like how Dr. Larry Taylor says it in his booklet, "Things I learned from my Pastor": Taylor says; "Look at it this way, in ministry there are no interruptions just opportunities. In service to the Lord you have opportunities to minister the love of God to whomever God brings to you." If you're guided by the Holy Spirit, you'll be open to hearing and obeying His voice then adapting to where the Spirit leads you.

While it's good to have a schedule and be organized, don't become a slave to your plans. Perhaps God's plans are different than what you have planned. Maybe God's plan is for you to visit someone in the hospital or to share Christ with a stranger, or to spend extra time with your spouse and kids. Walking in the Spirit implies openness to having your schedule rearranged and believing that God will help you get done what he wants done.

That's not to imply you shouldn't be diligent and a good steward of your time. The effective Christian is well organized yet flexible. Organized yet able to change is the way the Holy Spirit works. Every believer must be ready to do whatever the Lord says, just like Philip who left where God was moving to go where God wanted him to

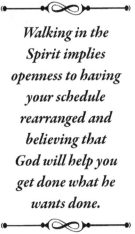

Walking in the Spirit implies openness to having your schedule rearranged and believing that God will help you get done what he wants done.

go. You should always be ready for whatever comes your way; whether blessing your family, teaching a Bible study, praying with someone, counseling, or jumpstarting someone's car. All of those things are ministry and all require flexibility.

If you're flexible, some people might not understand it, so just remember; they are not the one who heard from the Holy Spirit. Flexibility in following the Spirit means you have to learn to hear the Spirit's voice and as you do, following the Spirit is the most exciting way to live.

My first pastor, Dawson Wheeler, is perhaps the greatest evangelist I have ever known. Every day he speaks to people in the store or wherever he is and he leads many of them to Christ. Pastor Dawson always says; "You have to learn to recognize when the Holy Spirit is drawing someone. If they start a conversation with you; it may be the Spirit drawing them to you." So, every believer should always be ready to share the hope we have in Christ. *(1Peter 3:15).*

If you live a flexible life and learn to hear the Spirit's voice, then acting upon it you'll find joy and see much fruit because you're in the perfect will of God. Remember: Don't be so tied to your schedule that you miss what God wants you to do because, "The flexible never break."

CHALLENGE: Find a way to have a good schedule but make sure you know when you need to break your plans and follow what God has for you.

Chapter Five

GOD PROVIDES

Philippians 4:6 "Do not be anxious about anything, but in everything, by prayer and petition, with thanksgiving, present your requests to God."

Philippians 4:19 "And my God will meet all your needs according to His glorious riches in Christ Jesus."

Many have said; "Where God guides, God provides." In ministry it's not right to beg for money or manipulate people into giving. When churches beg for money it's usually because they're trying to build something other than what God has for them. If it's true; "Where God guides, He provides", could it also be true; "If He's not providing, maybe He's not guiding?"

Many a church has a bad reputation because they over-emphasize money and giving. If God is guiding the church, then they will be good stewards of God's finances and not overspend. As Chuck Smith used to say; "God doesn't need your money, He's not poor and the Kingdom of God is not about to go bankrupt." While that's true, people still need to learn the Biblical principles of giving so they can honor God and be blessed. It's just as true that a church should teach all the principles of giving but not make it central to every service. I believe you should address giving in a straightforward way whenever you teach the scriptures where giving is found.

Messages on giving cannot be a steady diet for the church nor should they only be given when the budget is low. Your motive should be to teach the whole counsel of God's Word, which includes messages on tithing. When your motives are God's motive, the result will be the people will be blessed. The church must have pure motives in all things, especially when it comes to finances, so, always check your motives but also teach God's motives. Teach God's motives because God's motive is faith and faith will lead to a blessing for those who test God in tithes and offerings *(Malachi 3:10)*.

While the church's motivations on giving need to be pure, at the same time you cannot ignore finances. Scripture says we are not to be; "Slothful in business." *(Romans 12:11 KJV)*

Good stewardship means to be careful with God's money, so frugality is vital to every Christian home and every ministry. As a pastor, I never want to know who gives what because I don't want to treat anybody differently than anyone else. Every church should set up an accountability system that's theft proof with checks and balances.

In the recording of tithes and offerings, and the deposits, the pastor should not be involved except as an overseer. The people serving in those positions should be carefully selected and of the highest integrity.

The same is true for spending, the church should have a system to purchase what's needed and that system should be both controlled and budgeted. All spending should be accounted for and used sparingly as the Lord directs. Even in minor purchases you should ask; "Do we really need it?" The same is true for our homes, in America consumerism is out of control, I think it is time for every Christian home to be wise in spending and make sure we are investing in God's kingdom.

In our church different ministries have their own credit card, with limits for each department and there are absolutely no cash advances allowed. Each month receipts are turned in and we review the statements to see what was spent and question anything which doesn't seem reasonable. This makes each ministry leader accountable for their area of ministry. And credit cards are paid off each month to avoid paying interest.

We have more than one person count the offerings and sign for their count, and the counters are rotated from time to time. The count is then checked by a different person as the deposit is made. When the giving is recorded and placed into the accounting system that becomes another check and balance. When writing checks, every check requires two signatures to ensure accountability in every area. Finally, I occasionally log into our online banking to see if there have been any expenditures which are questionable or out of line.

Every large expenditure is part of the annual budget and when a non-budgeted (non-emergency) item comes up during the year; we have the church board approve it before we make the purchase. We also have a giving summary in our church bulletin so each month any of our members can see where the church is financially. If there are questions, any of our giving members may see the church books at any time.

Being transparent and open about finances is important both in income and spending. Transparency in finances gives the church members confidence that things are being handled in a professional and honest manner. As God provides, every ministry within the church must be faithful and honest with God's provision and the church must be generous. At our church, we try to give away at least 10% of all that God provides. We give to missionaries around the world, relief organizations, as well as benevolence and outreaches both inside and out of the church. Believing that you can't out give God, we have seen the more we give, the more God provides.

Stewardship is just as important for the individual as for the church, every Jesus follower must be a good Steward of what God has provided. Debt is a terrible master and if you can't

> *As God provides, every ministry within the church must be faithful and honest with God's provision and the church must be generous.*

28

control your spending, life will be consumed with paying bills and never getting ahead and what good are you for the kingdom of God if your life is consumed by debt? So, every believer must live within their means and see themselves as Stewards of God's provision. Every Christian must believe what Jesus said; *Acts 20:35 ESV "...It is more blessed to give than to receive."* And every Christian must be taught the principles of tithing and generosity or they will not grow in their faith.

If you want to be involved in ministry you must be generous but at the same time live within your budget. Every budget should have the tithe and offerings as the first-fruits to be given to the Lord. Your home church should be the first place you send your tithe, then as God lays other needs on your heart you should support whatever ministry God shows you.

Being a generous and good Steward is vital to your faith so remember; A Steward is someone who's in charge of another's goods; therefore, all you have belongs to God. He provides so He should get the first-fruits of all you have.

CHALLENGE: If you have not been a good steward of God's money, come up with a plan and begin to trust God. If your church does not have accountability built into its systems, call the leaders together to create a system that's theft proof, generous and has checks and balances.

Chapter Six

HEALTHY THINGS GROW

John 15:16 "You did not choose me, but I chose you and appointed you to go and bear fruit — fruit that will last."

I t's been said; "Sheep beget sheep!" If you're walking with the Lord, it's essential you have a heart for the lost with a deep desire to evangelize and see missionary outreach around the world. Every congregation and every believer must catch the vision to reach the lost and be involved in missionary work, and evangelism. The primary responsibility of pastors and church leadership is to feed God's sheep and equip them for the work of the ministry.

Ephesians 4:11-12 ESV "And he gave the apostles, the prophets, the evangelists, the pastors and teachers, to equip the saints for the work of ministry, for building up the body of Christ."

Church leaders must prepare God's people for God's work. When a congregation is fed a good diet of the Word of God, and the whole counsel of God's word, they will be healthy and equipped for what God has for them. Just like healthy sheep automatically and naturally reproduce so it is with God's sheep. Healthy believers will share their faith and have a burden for the lost and that's good news for church leaders because they'll never have to pump the people up or have a special "invite your friend to church day" because evangelism will naturally take place. The principle is simple; Feed God's flock and they will reproduce because; "Healthy things grow."

Mission programs, evangelistic outreaches and benevolence are all vital to church life, but at the same time they are a by-product of solid Bible teaching. If a church wants to build a missions program it needs to start by feeding God's people, then outreach will be part of the fruit.

> *The principle is simple; Feed God's flock and they will reproduce because; "Healthy things grow."*

While evangelistic meetings are good and may bring some to faith, the reality is most people come to Christ by one on one encounters with a real, true believer. When you understand that truth, you'll see how investing in people by loving them, feeding them the Word of God and teaching them God's heart for the lost will produce the good fruit of souls for God's kingdom.

Back to our text in Ephesians, Paul reminds us of the purpose of church leadership. ***Ephesians 4:12 "To equip the saints for the work of ministry, for building up the body of Christ."*** Every church leader has the important calling to build up the body. Some leaders think it's their job to keep the body in line or to assert their authority over the body. The Spirit led leader is one who understands their job is to serve and build up and while there is a time and place for church discipline, the end result of discipline should be to build the people up thus most of your leadership should be about pointing people towards Jesus.

Pointing people to Jesus is something we get to do and is best done as we offer grace before judgement and place a higher standard on ourselves as leaders than we do on the people we are serving. No matter where you serve in the church, with the children, as an usher or in the kitchen, you must have a heart for people who do not know the Lord. While some have a special gift of evangelism, every Christian must have a heart for the lost and be able to present the gospel in both their actions and their words.

CHALLENGE: Ask yourself when was the last time you shared your faith? When was the last time your church talked about evangelism? What type of leader are you, one who builds up or one who exerts their authority?

Chapter Seven

BE LOYAL AND SUBMISSIVE

Titus 3:1 "Remind the people to be subject to rulers and authorities, to be obedient, to be ready to do whatever is good."

As Aaron and Hur worked alongside of Moses they helped as they stood by his side and held his arms up in battle. That's a great picture of your responsibility towards those God has placed over you. Your role is to ease the burden of those over you in the Lord. You make their job lighter by holding up their arms and helping them in any way you can.

How can you help? First, pray for those you serve with, encourage them, and provide lots of information to them so they can know what's going on and won't be surprised by anything. Provide input and opinion to support them, but remember, no leader needs a "yes man" nor do they need someone who causes division. If God has placed someone over you, submit to them, love them, pray for them and help them. Above all, always be loyal and never betray those with whom you minister. Never back-bite, publicly criticize, or gossip about them. If you see something in their life or ministry that's not right, speak the truth to them but do it in love and do it in such a way as to bring about healing and restoration.

Above all, always be loyal and never betray those with whom you minister.

The principle of submission applies to all of life just as much as ministry. In marriage we are called to bring love and respect to one another and that's demonstrated by being honest, open and loyal to one another. *(Ephesians 5:33)* In the workplace the Christian is called to serve those in authority and recognize its Christ you're serving. *(Ephesians 6:5-8)*

In a marriage we are called to endure because Christ has joined us together, but in ministry if there's something you can't live with, leave quietly and don't try to build another ministry by causing division. Remember, the Bible says; "Touch not the Lord's anointed." *(Psalm 105:15)* If a church leader is "out to lunch", God will deal with them. Remember the example from David? David waited patiently for God to remove Saul even though he knew Saul was not trusting God nor serving God's people.

Your job in ministry should never be the cause of strife or division. Instead, you get to help, encourage, submit, assist and lighten the load by serving those over you. That's how you serve God, by serving those God has placed over you. If you're doing your ministry right, then those over you will never worry about what's entrusted to you. That's real unity when every leader has confidence that the ministry is running the way it should be.

> *Ephesians 5:21 "Submit to one another out of reverence for Christ."*

CHALLENGE: Examine your loyalty to see if you have been bucking those over you. If you have, repent and confess it than begin to support them.

> *Psalm 133:1 "Behold, how good and pleasant it is when brothers dwell in unity!" ESV*

Chapter Eight

EMPHASIZE WHAT GOD HAS DONE

Romans 5:8 "But God demonstrates his own love for us in this: While we were still sinners, Christ died for us."

1 John 4:10 "In this is love, not that we loved God, but that He loved us and sent His Son to be the propitiation for our sins."

In preaching and teaching, our priority should be to speak about what God has done for us and not what we can do for God. Grace is the heart of the Gospel, because grace is the unmerited, unearned favor of God. God, in grace, pours out love and forgiveness to those who deserve judgement, so we must teach, preach and live out grace every day. As Jesus followers we should always try to error on the side of grace especially when dealing with tough issues. If you lean toward Grace whenever possible, you'll never be overly harsh with people. If you lean toward extending Grace whenever you can, you will always be extending what God has extended to you.

Today many in ministry seem to emphasize what the people need to do for God – give more money, pray more, study harder, or volunteer more. When you emphasize those things, it could discourage people because those things can become a law unto themselves.

> *Galatians 2:16 ESV "...We know that a person is not justified by works of the law but through faith in Jesus Christ, so we also have believed in Christ Jesus, in order to be justified by faith in Christ and not by works of the law, because by works of the law no one will be justified."*

The heart of the Gospel always emphasizes what God has already done for us; Jesus loves us, He died for us, He rose from the grave, ascended to the right hand of the Father where He ever lives to make intercession for us. He has forgiven all our sins and abides with those who love Christ. He has empowered us with His Spirit, who is always there to help us, guide us and prepare us for our eternal reward. And oh yes, don't forget; Jesus is coming again to judge the living and the dead. A Grace driven life will remember Jesus is coming again, so consistent reminders of the

The heart of the Gospel always emphasizes what God has already done for us.

rapture of the church and the resurrection of the dead are important parts of presenting grace.

If you emphasize what we do for God, that becomes a burden people can never meet, but when you speak of what God has done for us, that is when your service to God becomes a response to what He has done for us. As we teach what God has done for us, people's hearts will overflow with gratitude. Those involved in frontline ministry get to lead people past their problems and into the arms of Jesus and that is best done by showing and teaching love and grace.

Similarly, in counseling it's easy to train people to rely on the counseling rather than relying on the Lord. Because you want people to go to Christ first, it's important to emphasize God's loving grace and let them see Jesus clearly. To do that you must always use Biblical counseling because whenever you go to the Scriptures for answers, you'll always see God's heart on whatever the issue is. Personally, I believe the Bible provides answers for anything we face in life either directly or indirectly.

> *2 Peter 1:3 ESV "His divine power has granted to us all things that pertain to life and godliness, through the knowledge of him who called us to his own glory and excellence."*

Most likely you are not trained in psychology and even if you are, the word of God is more powerful than human wisdom. So, pointing people to Jesus and using the examples of Scripture to guide them is the most powerful way to counsel.

The purpose of the church must represent what God has done for us! I believe the right vision for every ministry should be;

1. **To Worship God**
2. **To build up the People**
3. **To Evangelize the World**

While most Bible believing churches have all three of these elements in their vision statement, I believe this is the proper order. Why do I think that's the right order? Because we are created to worship God, and it's the church's responsibility to build people up through teaching the Word, whereby equipping them to go into all the world to share the gospel. *(Ephesians 2:10)*. When your priorities are lined up with God's plan you will always be pointing people to what God has done and as you do, you will create healthy Jesus followers.

Seeing Jesus clearly should be the goal of every service, every study, every program and every gathering. That means even a fun time such as a harvest festival or open gym night there should be an opportunity to present the Gospel. The church must keep our main focus to represent Christ in our culture and when every activity we have centers on the Gospel, we will be seen as Christ's ambassadors.

As you speak about what God has done for mankind, people will see God's love and their response will be a desire to see the lost come to faith and a deeper walk for those who are saved.

> *"How great is the love the Father has lavished on us, that we should be called children of God...!"*
> *(1 John 3:1)*

CHALLENGE: Look at your life and ministry and ask; Do I emphasize rules and human action or Grace and what God has done for us?

Chapter Nine

FEED GOD'S SHEEP

John 21:15 "...Jesus said to Simon Peter, "Simon, son of Jonah, do you love Me more than these?" He said to Him, "Yes, Lord; You know that I love You." He said to him, "Feed My lambs."

Jesus never said to beat the Sheep, yet some in ministry rebuke people and lay guilt trips on them for what they are not doing. If that's what people receive from church leaders it will result in condemnation and that church is not representing Christ.

God didn't allow Moses to enter the Promised Land, in part because he misrepresented the Lord. Moses gave the people the impression God was mad at them when He wasn't. Moses beat the rock in anger and broke the pattern of Christ being bruised one time and the result was he never walked into the promises of God. We learn from that event how those in ministry must be careful not to misrepresent God. God is not mad at His people and if you, as a leader are, you need to get back in touch with the Lord.

When you feed God's people by teaching them the entire Word of God and speak the truth in love to them, they should grow and see Jesus clearly. Of course, there will always be some people who no matter how well fed they are with God's word, they may never apply it. But in general, when believers are given a good diet of God's living and active Word, and they're shown an example of grace, they will grow.

> *2 Timothy 3:16-17 "All Scripture is God-breathed and is useful for teaching, rebuking, correcting and training in righteousness, so that the man of God may be thoroughly equipped for every good work."*

Let the Bible do what it does so well, teach, rebuke, correct and train in righteousness as it equips God's people. While there's always a temptation to preach to those who are not there, it's a very silly thing to do. Why rant and rave about commitment to the ones who showed up for service? Forget about who's not there and lovingly feed those who are and you'll see the ministry grow.

When a church is smaller, there's also a temptation for pastors to preach on a topic because they know some things about the people. All preaching and teaching must be Spirit led because that's when God speaks even to those who you think need to hear "your special message." Guard your heart and watch your motives because the only legitimate motive is love. Love is why you teach, why you preach, why you worship and love is why you serve. If you love Jesus you will love His people and you will be a faithful Shepherd. And pastoral ministry is not just for pastors, everyone with any authority in the church is pastoring those under them. We get to be faithful under shepherds to those God has entrusted to us.

I believe the best way to feed God's people is to teach the Bible. The best way I find to teach the Bible is to go through it book by book. Although I preach topical series from time to time, I believe expositional teaching is best as it brings out the context of every scripture used in teaching. If you go through an entire book of the Bible you should always focus on the context of the book as that helps the passages mean more by under-standing the way they were orig-inally given. Believers grow as they understand the meaning of the text and not just hear a sermon that ties one verse to a topic.

> *I believe the best way to feed God's people is to teach the Bible.*

When teaching in the Old Testament, the best way to approach scripture is to present Jesus, so you look for Jesus in every passage. Hermeneutics is the science of Biblical interpretation; I like what Pastor Jon Courson says about it; "The best hermeneutic is; 'Him-a-nutic'". Look for Him, looking for Jesus in every passage because you will find Him in the Law, the Passover, the Water that came from the Rock and the Brass Serpent Moses made. We see Moses, Joseph and David are all types of Christ, so always look for Jesus even within the Old Covenant. When you look for Jesus in all of scripture, you'll always emphasize what God has done, because He loved the world so much, He gave us His Only Son.

When teaching the Old Testament, remember, the New Testament always interprets the Old Testament. It is the fulfillment of it and many times we find quotations from the Old in the New and that's the proper interpretation of the passage.

> **Romans 11:36 "For from Him and through Him and to Him are all things. To Him be the glory forever! Amen."**
>
> **1 John 4:19 ESV "We love because he first loved us."**

CHALLENGE: Read your favorite Old Testament passages and look for Jesus within those scriptures.

Chapter Ten

GOD'S WORD HAS POWER

Jeremiah 3:15 "Then I will give you shepherds after my own heart, who will lead you with knowledge and understanding."

Isaiah 55:11 "So is my word that goes out from my mouth: It will not return to me empty, but will accomplish what I desire and achieve the purpose for which I sent it."

Hebrews 4:12 "For the word of God is living and active. Sharper than any double-edged sword, it penetrates even to dividing soul and spirit, joints and marrow; it judges the thoughts and attitudes of the heart."

You can present the Word of God in a loving, relaxed, and relevant manner when you believe God's Word does not go out void but some preachers want to either yell at their people or bore them to death. Some like to preach messages that are deep intellectually but not relevant to life, while others lay guilt trips on people as they neglect showing the love and freedom we find in Christ.

All preaching and teaching should be balanced. In expositional teaching of books of the Bible, you cover many important topics over the course of time. If you only preach topically it's harder to keep from repeating the same themes and easy to overlook lesser doctrines. Even as Peter was called to feed the sheep, I find the best way to feed God's people is to teach the entirety of the Bible in context, line upon line and verse by verse. This brings balance to my preaching and keeps me from getting off on pet doctrines. When I preach through the Bible, I can say with the Apostle Paul; "I've declared the whole counsel of God" *(Acts 20:27)*.

When people are fed God's word on a consistent basis, they should grow and produce good fruit. God is seeking leaders who will feed His people and who will stick to what the Bible actually says without adding to it. Sadly, today there are many who want to tickle the ears of their listeners instead of preaching the truth.

I've found that staying current on the times keeps my studies relevant. I like to scatter throughout my preaching information on current affairs, prophecy, the political climate, social problems, evidence for creation, and alike. Bible teachers should read magazines, newspapers and search the internet to stay informed, while avoiding extremes and conspiracy theories.

I believe every sermon should follow the 4 M's.

1. **Milk:** That's the simple truth found in the text you're preaching.
2. **Meat:** That's something to challenge the mature believer.
3. **Manna:** Is the application for the text.
4. **Marker:** Always pointing people to Jesus, He's the marker.

As you present God's word in these ways, you will grow the immature, challenge the mature and point everyone to the one who has all the answers, Jesus. Another important test for preaching is what our Lutheran friends say; "Every sermon should contain, Law and Gospel." I agree when you present Law you must present Gospel, because the Law condemns but the Gospel gives freedom. Still, I'm not convinced that every sermon must have the two, because sometimes you're preaching has little to do with salvation but may be about spiritual growth.

As you present God's Word you should do it in a relaxed manner, as you do everyone will feel welcome; those from different church backgrounds, varying ages, even the unsaved. While informality is inviting, it's important to not offend your audience, so your dress and your language should be appropriate for the demographic you are speaking to. The Apostle Paul says it the best;

> *1 Corinthians 9:19-23 "Though I am free and belong to no man, I make myself a slave to everyone, to win as many as possible. To the Jews I became like a Jew, to win the Jews. To those under the law I became like one under the law (though I myself am not under the law), so as to win those under the law. To those not having the law I became like one not having the law (though I am not free from God's law but am under Christ's law), so as to win those not having the law. To the weak I became weak, to win the weak. I have become all things to all men so that by all possible means I might save some. I do all this for the sake of the gospel, that I may share in its blessings."*

Even as Paul said; he becomes all things to all people so he might win some, so you never want to offend or distract from the power of God's Word by something as simple as how you dress or your vocabulary. I always say; "You don't wear a suit to witness at the Skate Park". In other words, dress, speak and act appropriately for those you are addressing, because that's the best way to win as many as possible. And don't be so informal in dress that you offend those who are more proper. Years ago, we had a man who would wear a tie to church each Sunday, when some guys who always wore Levis started to give him a hard time, I wore a tie to church for the next year. I never want exteriors such as dress or jargon to offend anyone, so know your audience, and dress and speak in a way to not offend, but to win as many as possible.

When teaching on a topic always use scripture as the launching pad for your message. When you begin with a premise or a topic you will be scattered in how you present it, even if you fill it with scripture references. But when you use a particular scripture as your "home base" you are saying you believe the power is in God's Word. God's Word will not return void but will accomplish the purpose for which it is intended. Too often I have heard topical messages where scripture is almost an afterthought or even non-existent. While the topic might be important and relevant, remember, the power is in the Word of God and not your delivery! It's been said that Jonathan Edwards actually read his famous sermon "Sinners in the Hands of an Angry God", and look at what God did with that, many came to Christ the day he preached it and many more though the ages have come to faith because of Edward's ministry.

When you believe God's Word has power, everything you do in ministry will focus on the Word. When you counsel, as you speak, and when you preach, remember, like Peter said to Jesus;

John 6:68 "...Lord, to whom shall we go? You have the words of eternal life."

In today's church, it's sad to say that while many claim they believe God's Word, very few act as if the Word has power, so they rely on techniques, programs and emotionalism. Those can easily become a substitute for the only place we can go to find the power of life and death. God's word will never go out void, and our job is to proclaim it and recognize it will do what God said it will do. You must believe that God has given us the canon of Scripture and the words in your Bible are 100% inspired by God and without error in their original language.

One of the most powerful services I was ever part of was a New Year's Eve service where we read the book of Revelation without comment. We worshiped between the chapters and we saw the power of God work as the only words spoken were right from scripture. When you believe in the power of the word of God and believe the canon of Scripture is inspired by God you will always make sure that God's Word is proclaimed and you will see much fruit in your ministry.

CHALLENGE: Do you really believe the Bible is the Word of God? Do you really act and teach like the Bible is God's Word? If not, I suggest you read the gospels and make the changes that show you believe that God's Word has power.

Chapter Eleven

TEACH THE WORD

2 Timothy 2:15 KJV "Study to shew thyself approved unto God, a workman that needeth not to be ashamed, rightly dividing the word of truth."

This chapter is really a continuation from the previous chapter but it's so important I felt we need to look at it in a different light.

Those who believe in Biblical inerrancy must look to the Bible as the literal Word of God. If you believe the Bible is God's word and it has power and if you are going to be used by God, you must focus on the Word of God and understand sound doctrine. The person God uses must study the Bible in order to show himself approved. The one who handles the Word correctly is the one who is able to not only give an answer for the hope they have, but is able to minister to whomever God brings into their life.

Preparation for teaching and preaching is vital. Preparation must begin with prayer allowing God to guide your studies. Next, you prepare as you study out the text, and (as stated in the previous chapter) I believe every sermon, every teaching should center on a Biblical text. While it is good to teach a principle, it's important to begin with a "home scripture" and build on it the lessons to be taught. This principle not only applies to Pastors but to Sunday School teachers and small group leaders as well.

Today we are blessed to have many excellent Bible translations and by simply reading your text in the different translations you'll gain a greater understanding of the text. I find my Bible software program is a great tool to help compare translations but there are excellent websites to help with this as well.

While every Bible teacher has their favorite translations, and I certainly have mine, I would simply say, do some research to find the most accurate translations and only use Bible paraphrases as commentary and do not teach them as an accurate translation. For those who get caught up in the "King James only" school I would say, get off the internet sites that promote controversy and do some real research on the science of Biblical translation.

I believe using scripture to prove scripture is the best way to teach a principle because the power is in God's Word; it's alive and living and never returns void. Scripture references cannot be seen as just sermon filler but they too accomplish the purpose God intended for them.

2 Timothy 3:16-17 "All scripture is God-breathed and is useful for teaching, rebuking, correcting and training in righteousness, so that the man

of God may be thoroughly equipped for every good work."

Another benefit to scripture references in teaching is that it gives a constant reminder of the harmony of Scripture. Old and New Testament alike speak of the God who loves us so much that He sent His only Son to die for our sins. All of Scripture works together to show us the whole plan of God to redeem those who are held captive by sin. Scripture will teach, rebuke, correct, train in righteousness and equip every believer for the good work God has for them, so we use scripture because the power is not in your presentation but in the proclamation of God's word.

When preparing for a message, I write out my notes. Although many excellent preachers do not – for me, writing them out does three things. First, it prepares me; the words to be spoken to the congregation are in my heart and on my mind. I never just read my notes, but I do write them out so I know where I'm going in the message and if I am doing multiple services there is a consistency to each of the services. Secondly, it keeps me current; I have an aid that keeps me from using an illustration too often. While every preacher has a tendency to repeat things which have blessed them, by writing out your message you will keep the things you share fresh and not use the

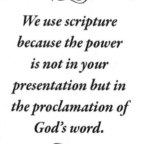

We use scripture because the power is not in your presentation but in the proclamation of God's word.

same old illustrations. Thirdly, I have a personal commentary; in writing out the messages I have preached throughout the years, I have created a huge library and personal commentary for the entire Bible. Now I am able, in a reasonable amount of time, to prepare a message for just about any book of the Bible or topic. Although I never preach the exact same message again, I do use the older messages as a "seed document" to prepare the new one.

I find another helpful key to message preparation is, to title the sermon. Even in expositional teaching a sermon title keeps me focused in my studies and helps convey the main message I feel the Lord wants to speak. With my message having a title, I stay focused on what I feel God wants me to say. As I prepare, I can make sure every illustration, every reference, and every point made, ties to the main theme of the message. I do this by continually asking myself; "How does this relate to what God wants me to say?"

Speaking of illustrations, I find it important not to use my own life experiences too often. Yes, it's good to be candid and open with people, but if I tell too many personal stories people will get tired of them and will even predict what story I'm going to tell. I was in a church for a few years where I could tell you exactly what the pastor was going to say or what story he was going to tell. I have visited my adult children's church a few times and each time the pastor told the same story, so even as a visitor I lost interest. When giving any illustration make sure it is more about God than yourself. When any sermon or teaching is finished, the people should know more about God than they do about the teacher. I can recall a funeral I attended where the Pastor and the deceased were good friends but by the end of the service, I knew more about the Pastor than the departed.

Good illustration management is another important topic. Writing out your sermons helps, but a simple log on your computer or even a hard copy with the dates used, will help keep great illustrations from becoming stale and overused.

Using props, physical things or even videos to make an illustration can be a very effective tool in preaching and teaching but they can also become a burden if you over use them. I try to limit the use of physical illustrations to keep them from becoming old hat or making them something I have to come up with, or something that could potentially distract from good Bible teaching.

I visited a large church where every week they used props to illustrate the message being given. The week I was there I felt what they did distracted from the message and it felt like more effort was put into the example than the message. Having said that, I like using a PowerPoint presentation with a simple outline to show how things tie together and having major scripture references on a slide keeps things flowing without a lot of awkward silence. Although I use a presentation, I never want to be a slave to so I don't always use one, but I do recognize it helps the "note takers" with their notes and it becomes a visual aid to how things tie together.

Humor can be a powerful tool which God can use to make people comfortable while highlighting an important or heavy principle. But the use of humor for humor's sake is a place where pride can come into play. There's always a temptation to try to be funny when it just might be the time for serious words. Allister Begg once said; "You are not called to be cleaver or entertaining but you are called to be faithful to God's word." Our flesh loves to get accolades and be pumped up, so being cleaver in presenting a message is one area you must check your pride. As your focus is on teaching the Word, even if you use humor to communicate, you should always check your motive and purpose in saying anything that can distract from the power of God's Word.

When using humor, the best advice I ever received was from a man who is very funny. Gayle D. Erwin is the author of "The Jesus Style" and a teacher to pastors. Gayle says; when using humor it should always be for a purpose and you should be careful when telling a joke, especially jokes which have a butt to them where someone could get hurt. He says; it's better to look for humor in the Bible text or life itself. You can find a lot of humor in the Bible, whether it's the Apostles who were always bickering about their own self-worth, or Gideon who's the most reluctant of leaders, or Jonah who ran away from God, etc. The Bible is full of humorous stories and characters and finding the humor in God's Word can be very effective.

Looking for humor in life events is also a very effective way to communicate. There are a lot of funny things happening along the way to heaven and whether it's from your experiences or someone else's, using the humor of life helps people relate to whatever you are talking about.

Another good approach to humor is to use yourself as the butt of your humor. Putting yourself down is safe while putting others down is not safe because even if the person is not offended by your joking, someone else may hear it and be put off. The purpose of humor should always be to highlight a point and to put people at ease in order to receive an important spiritual principle. If your use of humor offends or turns someone off, it's better to be serious and let them hear the truth.

I believe it's important to cover a book in the Old Testament from time to time. If we're going to emphasize what God has done, we must preach Jesus and Jesus is in the New Testament. But the Old Testament is full of pictures and prophecies about the Lord as well. Using the entire Bible builds a strong congregation and helps people to learn how all of scripture is "God breathed."

The purpose of humor should always be to highlight a point and to put people at ease in order to receive an important spiritual principle.

Even when teaching children, it's important to give the Old Testament lessons so they too can see how all the Bible ties to the one great message of God's great love for us. Once a guy told me we should never teach children the Ten Commandments, because that's the Old Covenant. How wrong was that! The Commandments are what reveal our sin and draw us to grace, they also show us the heart of God and what a life of holiness looks like.

In our church the mid-week service focuses primarily on the Old Testament and our Sunday services on the New. Although that model works for me, it is not "cast in stone" and I believe preaching from the Old Testament as well as the New is important and can be very helpful in building a well-rounded congregation.

The use of jargon, slang and even how you dress should be appropriate for your audience. Why would you want to lose your hearers by how you speak or what you wear? So be aware of your audience and become what you must to win all you can.

Today more than ever, the use of "Church Language" is less effective than ever. Phrases like; "pressing in, under the blood, bathed in prayer, or hedge of protection" are not understood by new believers or those still seeking. If you must use a term which only the churched are going to understand, take a second and explain it. This helps the younger believers to grow and the seekers to understand. Still finding a new way to communicate those principles is a great way to teach a godly concept without losing your audience.

> *2 Timothy 4:2-5 "Preach the Word; be prepared in season and out of season; correct, rebuke and encourage — with great patience and careful instruction. For the time will come when men will not put up with sound doctrine. Instead, to suit*

their own desires, they will gather around them a great number of teachers to say what their itching ears want to hear. They will turn their ears away from the truth and turn aside to myths. But you, keep your head in all situations, endure hardship, do the work of an evangelist, discharge all the duties of your ministry."

The time is now when people will not put up with sound doctrine. We have liberal churches that reduced scripture to a guideline and have dissected pages from the Bible which they believe "haven't evolved with the culture." They call good evil and evil good and so they will not put up with sound Biblical teaching. But there are also itching ears in churches which reduce ministry to a formula. They hold to the idea that if you get people in the church, at any cost, somehow, they will come to true faith. Some churches center on entertainment, others water down the Bible by avoiding hard doctrine or not addressing sins that the culture says are acceptable. Many people will never grow in their faith because their church is robbing them of the whole counsel of God's Word.

In preaching and teaching you should never be afraid to use doctrinal terms and words. Today there is a trend to dumb down a sermon thinking the church isn't ready for big words or large principles and that attitude causes many pastors to avoid doctrinal words and shorten their message. As you speak of Grace, Regeneration, Justification, Imputation, Sanctification, Propitiation, even Predestination and

Election and do so on a consistent basis, you will teach the congregation to think and to help them grow in their faith.

While sermons should be concise, you should never think that it has to be short or spoken at a child's level. If you believe your people want to worship God and want to grow in their faith, you will feed them the deeper things of God's Word and you will see them grow. Remember; *"Faith comes by hearing the Word of God" (Romans 10:17)* But faith does not come from your clever speech, so be concise as possible but don't be afraid of going deep.

One final thought, education! I believe it is important to continue your education and learning throughout your life. That may involve formal schooling, seminars, conferences or personal study. Those in ministry should always be growing in their understanding of scripture and doctrine.

I believe a well-rounded ongoing learning experience helps prepare you for life and ministry. That includes non-biblical education, English and history classes, and even business classes are very helpful in ministry. Of course, seminary and Bible college level classes are of utmost importance for those who want to grow in their own faith and ministry. While some would speak of seminary as a place that takes away from one's faith, reality is there are many godly schools that help those who want to serve the Lord and continue to grow in their faith and knowledge of the Lord Jesus.

I know a pastor who discourages young people from going to Bible College or Seminary. He refuses to read anything except the Bible and brags about his own lack of formal education. Not only does his church not grow, but we have had several people attend our church because they were so put off by his rhetoric and uneducated understanding of scripture. Be that as it may, if you want to be used by God, read, study and continue your education, either formal or personal, but understand that the person God uses understands you must continue to grow as a person as well as in your knowledge of God and ministry.

CHALLENGE: Examine your life and areas of ministry to see if you truly believe; "Faith comes by hearing the Word of God." Ask yourself if you understand doctrinal terms and if not study up and see how that knowledge will help you grow in your faith. Also examine your learning, is it ongoing or do you think you've arrived in your education?

Chapter Twelve

WORSHIP IS VITAL

Ephesians 5:18-20 "...Be filled with the Spirit. Speak to one another with psalms, hymns and spiritual songs. Sing and make music in your heart to the Lord, always giving thanks to God the Father for everything, in the name of our Lord Jesus Christ."

B eing filled with the Spirit results in a life of worship and while worship is vital to the life of the church it can easily become a distraction in the church.

Psalm 100:4-5 Enter his gates with thanksgiving, and his courts with praise! Give thanks to him; bless his name! For the Lord is good; his steadfast love endures forever, and his faithfulness to all generations. ESV

Corporate worship should not be considered the warm up for the sermon but actually and literally, entering into

God's presence and coming through His gates with thanksgiving and into His courts with praise. Jesus said;

> *"The Father seeks those who would worship Him in Spirit and in truth." (John 4:23, paraphrase mine)*

The chief purpose of the church is to worship God. Worship is much more than music, yet music and singing are one of the main ways we express worship in a congregational setting. Worship should be Spirit led and that has nothing to do with the style of music. In ministry we set an atmosphere and model for the congregation to participate in worship because true, heart felt, Spirit filled worship is vital as it prepares our hearts and makes us ready for what God wants to say.

Today the church is often filled with performance type music where the congregation is just watching a really "tight band" with great music. In Spirit led worship there's no need for smoke, overbearing lighting and sound or hyping the people up because in corporate worship we are leading the congregation into the presence of God. Whatever style of music your church is inclined toward should have no effect on Spirit led worship because you recognize that music and singing are not synonymous with worship, but they are part of true worship. In worship we offer our bodies (lives) as living sacrifices, so worship is lived out each day by all believers as we surrender to Jesus.

In corporate worship, church leaders should model to the people what it's like to enter into God's presence. Even if you are not outgoing in your personality or a good singer, your participation or nonparticipation in congregational worship is still noticed by the people. I know some pastors who sit in their office during song service then show up on stage to preach. Their actions say; congregational worship is not important and they are modeling that to their people. Leaders should be involved in corporate worship by teaching worship in both word and action.

Worship songs should be chosen carefully with words that speak truth and are honoring to God. There are a lot of songs, both older hymns and newer contemporary songs, where the words are not doctrinally sound. But there are also a lot of songs (both old and new) where the music is not very good. We find some songs with strong words that are hard to sing in a congregational setting and others where the lyrics are weak but the tune is catchy. However, when we find songs which have both strong words and good music, those songs should be the mainstay of corporate worship. Why sing songs just because the music is good? Why sing songs that don't flow musically? And why sing songs that are not true? Every worship song should have a depth in what it says and if the tune is catchy, that's a bonus.

When leading congregational worship, it's important to have a familiarity about the music. If only a few people know the songs, then only a few will be singing. Those leading worship have a responsibility to lead the congregation into God's presence and you do that in many different ways. Praying, reading scriptures, how you arrange the song or actually inviting the church to join the worship team in singing, those are a few ways to lead the people in corporate worship.

When introducing a new song, first it's important to not have too many new songs. The idea of congregational singing is to get people to join in worship and not everyone is as quick to learn a new song as those who are musically inclined. A song may not feel new to you because you have practiced it and may have led the congregation in it once or twice, but it may be unfamiliar to many in the church, so be careful not to overload a day of worship with songs that the people don't know. When introducing a new song, it may be helpful to say something

Why sing songs that don't flow musically? And why sing songs that are not true? Every worship song should have a depth in what it says and if the tune is catchy, that's a bonus.

about it or go over the chorus before leading the church. This too is an invitation to join in worship that teaches the church the importance of congregational singing.

Worshiping God will be the priority in heaven, so worship is vital here on earth. When leaders model worship to the congregation they show that they really believe;

Psalm 22:3 KJV "But thou art holy, O thou that inhabitest the praises of Israel."

One last thought, from the woman Jesus spoke to in Samaria;

John 4:23-25 ESV (Jesus said to her) "But the hour is coming, and is now here, when the true worshipers will worship the Father in spirit and truth, for the Father is seeking such people to worship him. God is spirit, and those who worship him must worship in spirit and truth."

What an important truth; that God is seeking after worshipers, so the Bible tells us we were created for His pleasure, and we're to give Him honor. Those who worship rightly will worship in both spirit and truth. In other words, right worship will involve our spirits touching God's Spirit and right worship will always involve truth. Music can stir the emotions and quiet your soul, when a congregation participates in corporate worship in singing; they are entering into the courts of God through the medium of music.

CHALLENGE: Be in constant examination of your corporate worship. Look closely at the songs that are sung to see if the meet the criteria of Spirit and Truth. Also examine your personal worship, are you moved by the type of song and the quality of the band or do you sing unto the Lord? Are you a model to others of a worshiper or do you just tolerate the song service?

Psalm 149:1 ESV "Praise the Lord! Sing to the Lord a new song, his praise in the assembly of the godly!

Chapter Thirteen

BE BALANCED

1 Timothy 4:16 "Watch your life and doctrine closely. Persevere in them, because if you do, you will save both yourself and your hearers."

I believe the church should try to avoid issues that tend to divide the Body of Christ, as Chuck Smith once said; "When Christ's Body is divided, pray tell, who bleeds?"

Being balanced in theology means you avoid the extremes of Pentecostalism and Fundamentalism. Pentecostalism is full of emotionalism and an emphasis on the gifts of the Spirit, often at the expense of the Word of God. While the other end of the spectrum is Fundamentalism with its opposition to the gifts of the Spirit. I believe a healthy church allows the operation of all the gifts of the Spirit, but always decently and in order. What does it mean to be in order? For our church it means the manifestational gifts are practiced only at a believers meeting. The Apostle Paul says it the best;

"If an unbeliever comes into your meetings and things are not in order, they will think you are nuts and be closed to the Gospel." 1Corinthians 14:24 (paraphrase mine).

Why would anyone want to limit their mission field by things that are not essential? Hence, I do not believe Sunday morning worship is the proper place for the manifestational gifts to operate. The Holy Spirit never interrupts Himself, so the gift of tongues should not be allowed while the Word is being taught.

Another extreme is found in the hyper-Calvinist who teaches that Jesus died only for His elect, that man has no free will and some are elect for heaven, while others elect for hell. Opposite them are the extreme Arminian churches that forget about the sovereignty of God and believe a person must be born again over and over again because they can lose their salvation every time they sin. It's important to be balanced in these areas because the Bible clearly teaches the sovereignty of God and the responsibility of man. We also see the security of the believer along with perseverance of the saints.

While we may never intellectually reconcile some Bible doctrines, we can accept the fact that God is bigger than we are, so we should teach all that the Bible says, while avoiding the extremes and the labels some groups want to put on everyone. I have found that the fruit of extreme Calvinism is argumentation and labeling other believers. While the fruit of extreme Arminianism, is insecurity. To be balanced theologically means you can avoid the labels and look for unity in the whole body of Christ. You can enjoy fellowship with Calvinists and learn from their passionate preaching. And you can enjoy friendship with those in the Arminian camp and glean from their passion for evangelism.

Other areas where some churches tend to get out of balance are seen when they preach social reform at the expense of the gospel. While good works are a result of waking with Jesus, we know that only the gospel gives hope beyond this life, so we must find balance with social causes that replace the gospel and evangelism.

Other groups focus on good causes such as; pro-life and still others constantly preach against certain sins like; homosexuality, or at the other end of the spectrum still others preach pop-psychology at the neglect of the Scriptures. When a church's focus is to prioritize those types of things, that's what they become known for. A church should not be known for what they are against or for preaching a watered-down gospel, but as Jesus said;

**"*All men will know you are my disciples by your love one for another." (John 13:35)*

Stay balanced and true to the Word of God, not neglecting the hard things while not overemphasizing the minor things. Not long ago I had a woman say to me that if I didn't speak about sins (such as homosexuality) the church would be larger. She had attended enough to know that I only spoke about such sins when they were in the scriptures we were studying. I told her I could not water down God's Word because someone was offended and she has never come back to our church. Remember, the Word of God will always be offensive to those with a hard heart.

The exact opposite is true for those churches that avoid hard topics and do not tie scripture to the world we live in. When you avoid speaking about social sins, or whitewash what the Bible says about things such as fornication, homosexuality, drunkenness or even gossip, you are not giving the people the heart of God. The churches that lean away from the inerrancy of Scripture and avoid hard issues are actually the churches that are NOT growing.

Never avoid a hard topic or doctrine just because it's not politically correct or because you're afraid to offend someone. I have found when I present those issues with balance, showing the context of where it is found in the Bible, and present them with grace and love, that's when we grow as a church. When we preach the hard things of God's Word, those are often the very messages God uses to draw those deep in sin.

While preaching hard topics, it's important to present them in a way that's appropriate for those you are speaking to. If you're teaching children, you certainly wouldn't want to be as graphic or blunt as if you were speaking to

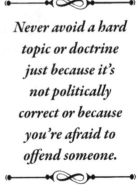

Never avoid a hard topic or doctrine just because it's not politically correct or because you're afraid to offend someone.

adults, once again the principle of knowing your audience is essential.

Today we find another disturbing trend where some want to divide the Bible into two parts with some parts seen as "more inspired" than others. If you believe in Biblical inerrancy, then you must view that the writings of Paul are just as inspired as the teachings of Jesus. You can't pick and choose which parts of the Bible are the most inspired. The only division in God's word is the division between the Old and New Covenant. Yet even the two Covenants work together to point us to the one Savior, Jesus.

> *2 Timothy 2:15 "Do your best to present yourself to God as one approved, a workman who does not need to be ashamed and who correctly handles the word of truth.*

If you're a workman for God, you are approved and you need to correctly handle, or "rightly divide" the Word of Truth. Christ has entrusted you with His Word, so be careful and balanced in how you present God's Word and you will find fruit in your ministry.

CHALLENGE: Ask yourself; do I have my "pet peeves", and find myself always teach against certain things? Do I talk about hard topics or avoid them? And how do others label me or my ministry? Do others see me as falling into a certain camp or just as a real follower of Jesus?

Chapter Fourteen

PRAYER

1 Samuel 12:23 "As for me, far be it from me that I should sin against the Lord by failing to pray for you. And I will teach you the way that is good and right."

Luke 21:36 "Be always on the watch, and pray that you may be able to escape all that is about to happen, and that you may be able to stand before the Son of Man."

Prayer is the lifeblood for every Christian and every ministry. It's been said; "The church moves forward on its knees." So, every successful ministry has dedicated prayer warriors behind it. While corporate prayer is the hardest ministry to keep strong, the reality is we must get our people praying and keep them praying.

Recently I was in a city with a large mosque located near my hotel. When they had the call to prayer, I saw men running to get to prayer. It was an interesting picture of their dedication to pray repetitive prayers and pray them to a god they cannot reach. If that's how those without Christ prioritize their time of prayer, how much more should the Church of the Living God make a priority of prayer? Sadly, corporate prayer meetings are often the least attended meetings in the church.

> ***Matthew 6:7 NLT (Jesus said) "When you pray, don't babble on and on as people of other religions do. They think their prayers are answered merely by repeating their words again and again."***

First Jesus said; "when you pray", not "if you pray", so according to Jesus praying is a must for the Christian. Then he said our prayers should not be babblings nor seen as a means to convince God to do what we want. No, prayer is the means by which we can participate in the will of God. And prayer is the channel through which He works as heartfelt believers touch the heart of God when they pray.

Every ministry and every home must be built on prayer. But remember even the Apostles had to ask Jesus; "Lord teach us to pray", in other words, prayer does not always come naturally but it's learned and like worship,

Prayer is the means by which we can participate in the will of God.

prayer must be modeled by church leaders.

Your personal prayer life is what keeps you in tune with the Spirit and helps you to bear the burdens of ministry, so as the bible says; *"Pray without ceasing!" (1 Thessalonians 5:17 NKJV)*. Then your personal prayer life must extend to your family; praying with your spouse on a regular basis and praying with your children whenever you can. In doing so you will not only model a healthy devotion to your family but you will be leading them as the Lord would have you lead. Lastly, church leaders should participate in corporate prayer. How can you expect your people to pray if you don't model it as important?

The great model for prayer in the bible is what we have called; "The Lord's Prayer".

Matthew 6:9-13 NKJV "In this manner, therefore, pray: Our Father in heaven, hallowed be Your name. Your kingdom come. Your will be done on earth as it is in heaven. Give us this day our daily bread. And forgive us our debts, as we forgive our debtors. And do not lead us into temptation, but deliver us from the evil one. For Yours is the kingdom and the power and the glory forever. Amen."

By using those scriptures as a guideline for your prayers, you'll find requests and intercessions flowing from the themes in the text. As you begin to pray, start with praise, then pray for God's will to be done in each situation that's on your heart. Ask for provision for those who need it as well as yourself. Then honestly confess your sin and ask for divine power to forgive those you need to forgive. Pray that you will be delivered from Satan's temptations and end just like you began, with praise to God. The wonderful thing about using the Lord's Prayer as your guide is, if you can't think of what to pray, it will prompt your heart to the needs deep within your soul.

Your posture in prayer is not important; you can pray standing, sitting, kneeling or even while jogging. In the Bible we see models of silent personal prayer, personal prayer, as well as corporate prayer. The position and the volume are not important but what's important is that our prayers are real and honest. I think that's why Jesus said go into your closet, shut the door and pray to your Father who sees your heart. In the closet with the door shut your prayers will be honest because it's just you and God. It's honest conversational prayer that connects us to God's heart and helps us to grow.

If someone comes to you with a burden, pray for them, right then. It doesn't matter if it's after the Sunday service and other people want to speak with you or when you are in the middle of your studies or some other task. If someone needs prayer, you should pray for them – right then. It doesn't matter if it's on the phone or in a restaurant, when you pray immediately, not only will you bless them, but you will also show them the power of prayer.

When praying in public, either at church or a community event, don't make your prayer a sermon. I find that invocations and benedictions that are pointed and concise are the most effective and who knows; you just might get invited back to pray another time. Even at church events, long public prayers distract from what God is doing and put the focus on the one praying instead of on the one we pray to.

I remember a marriage seminar Suzanne and I attended where the leader would pray for our meals with his booming voice. But he only used a few words saying; "There's a time to eat and a time to pray". I say "amen" to that, when you babble on or make your prayers into a sermon, you lose people and leave them with the impression that God hears you better because of how long or loud you pray. Sincere prayers need not be long but some people seem to think if they pray loud enough or long enough, they'll be heard better, but Jesus said otherwise.

> *Matthew 6:7-8 "And when you pray, do not keep on babbling like pagans, for they think they will be heard because of their many words. Do not be like them, for your Father knows what you need before you ask him."*

I believe the church should always offer prayer after the services. Those whom the Lord is calling need prayer, but so do the sick, hurting and lonely. I believe those called to prayer ministry should have oil ready to anoint the sick and pray the prayer of faith.

> *James 5:14 "Is any one of you sick? He should call the elders of the church to pray over him and anoint him with oil in the name of the Lord."*

When you learn to pray and model prayer to others, you will help develop a culture of prayer within the church. Prayer really is the lifeblood of the church, and it's essential to every home as well, so make prayer a priority in your own life, and then a priority in your home, finally, prayer should sustain every ministry in the church.

CHALLENGE: Consider how much personal prayer you have, and not being legalistic about the amount of time, examine how much you intercede for others and connect with the Lord. Also, ask yourself if you model prayer to those you serve with? Does your church see prayer as a priority and do you model it as important even to your family?

Chapter Fifteen

KNOW WHAT YOU KNOW

Proverbs 3:5-6 "Trust in the Lord with all your heart and lean not on your own understanding; in all your ways acknowledge him, and he will make your paths straight."

Larry Taylor says in "Things I learned from my pastor"; "When confronted with things you don't fully understand, fall back on what you do understand." Every mature Christian will face questions about things we might not fully understand. When you're confronted with those hard questions don't pretend to have all the answers. When there's a tragedy or heartache you may not have an answer, but you know there is comfort in prayer, God's word, and your presence. How can you answer the person who asks why? "Why did my child die?" "Why did my spouse leave?" "Why did I lose my job?" Those are real life questions that even a mature believer might face sooner or later.

When people come to you with unanswerable questions like; "Why did God allow this?" Or, "Why is this happening?" Sometimes your best response is to simply say; "I don't know" but then you should take them to those things you do know. You know God is good and that He loves us so much He sent Jesus. You know we can trust Him and when we do, He will direct us. You know Jesus will never leave us and we are headed for heaven and we know His Word is true. When confronted with hard things where the answers are not obvious don't respond with some cliché that gives little comfort. When people say things like; "he's in a better place", or "all things work for the good", although those things may be true to one degree or another, it is of little comfort for those hurting so much.

I believe a good model is found in Job's friends, who, when Job's troubles began, they sat with him in the ashes and didn't say a word *(Job 2:11-13)*. They started out good just being with their friend and not opening their mouths and saying something stupid. Later they began to say some things that were not very comforting, even accusing Job of unconfessed sin. James reminds us to be quick to listen and slow to speak *(James 1:19)*, and that's sound advice when you don't have the answers to people's problems.

We should always be real and honest and not pretend to be something we're not or pretend to understand things we don't. Not pretending to have all the answers, you can be yourself, be

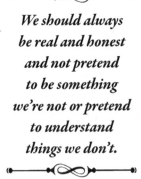

We should always be real and honest and not pretend to be something we're not or pretend to understand things we don't.

available, love God and love the people God has in your life. That's when you can be used even when things don't make sense. Remember, although there are some things we do not know, God through His Word, has given us what we need.

2 Peter 1:3 "His divine power has given us everything we need for life and godliness through our knowledge of him who called us by his own glory and goodness."

In other words, always take people to the Word of God then you can speak His revelation while avoiding speculation or popular sayings. When I'm confronted with hard things, sometimes I have to say; "I'm not sure, so let me get back to you." Although that's a great response, it means I have to get back with them in a timely manner. When I do, be it by text, email or in person, they appreciate my effort and I find that I grow personally from the study I put into the issue.

More important than what we do not know is Who we do know. So always point people to Jesus and always point them to the love of God. When dealing with tough issues it's important to understand, "we live in a fallen world" and sometimes that's the best answer for why things happen.

CHALLENGE: Look at how you respond to tough questions. Are you pointing people to Jesus? Do you pretend to know it all? Do people see you as empathetic or as cold? Is your reputation that of being loving and kind, or unavailable and too busy?

Chapter Sixteen

BE FAITHFUL TO YOUR CALLING

(John 14-16 & The Pastoral Epistles)

You may never be a pastor, the best speaker or the most dynamic personality but if you strive to love the people God has in your life, you will be a faithful shepherd to them. A shepherd is what every mature believer is when they minister to others. You may not have a title but you are a pastor to them in the sense that you're helping them become a disciple of Christ.

Love, of course, is the greatest gift and when you love God's people and do it by speaking the truth from the Word of God you are acting as Christ's ambassador. When your actions and words demonstrate love, that's the greatest gift you can give anyone.

The High priest of Israel had on his breast, stones that represented the 12 tribes *(Exodus 28:21)*. The Apostle Paul carried the believers on his heart *(2Corinthians 11:28)*. So, every pastor, every church leader and every parent should carry God's children on their heart. As you love them, serve them and feed them the Word of God, that's how you demonstrate love in the most powerful way.

Just as a Shepherd cares for his flock, so sacrifice is part of ministry. In service to God's people you get to sacrifice your time and desires as you fulfill God's calling in your life. You get to serve Christ's church with love and care as you serve His people. As you serve them your heart will be for them and that's when you are acting like a real shepherd and not someone that's only looking for prestige, position or power. When you're called to ministry, your heart must be for the people of God, and, you should see them like Christ sees them; as sheep who need a shepherd. A true shepherd is a leader who will not give up and leave the ministry when things are tough. It's been said that "ministry is like marriage", things can get tough from time to time but when you're called to it you won't abandon it. So true Shepherds won't give up on people, just as Jesus said, the good Shepherd leaves the ninety-nine to pursue the one lost sheep, so church leaders must be dispensers of mercy over and over again. I'm not saying that there's not a time for discipline or going separate ways, but every leader must lean towards mercy and grace even to the point that you believe it's better to error on the side of grace, than to condemn someone who's failed. Because God has called you to represent Him and Grace is what He has extended to you so you must extend mercy and grace to others.

In recent years several mega-church pastors have been ousted from their ministries because of heavy handed leadership. If you find yourself frustrated, angry with or lashing out at those you are serving, it's time to examine what you're doing. Jesus only rebuked those who were living in hypocrisy while he was kind but truthful to those caught in sin. If you're being harsh with those God has entrusted to your care, it's time to take a break and examine what you're doing and why you're in ministry.

If God has called you to a ministry (no matter how small or large) then that calling should become the motivation for ministry. When I say ministry, I mean anything where you're serving God by serving others. In the church, it may be teaching the children, helping with sound, cleaning toilets or any number of things, if God has called you, then be faithful to your calling.

Serving God's people should not come at the neglect of your own family and your own wellbeing. Many in ministry have what has been called "a savior complex", where they feel as if God's work won't happen without them. You're not the savior, and God has done his work for a long time without you! Just like Jesus found time to get alone and pray, so you must nurture both your own relationship with God and lead yourself and your family to Christ. Even as the requirements for church leaders tell us, those in ministry must lead their family well *(1 Timothy 3:4-5)*.

Leading yourself and your family requires time spent with the Lord and time spent with your spouse and kids. A faithful shepherd cares for God's people and recognizes their calling is to disciple others and help them grow in the Lord. At the same time a faithful leader understands that they cannot lead others where they have not gone themselves. You must keep your own relationship with God and your family strong if you are going to lead others.

Knowing there will be hard times and knowing sometimes people will break your heart, you won't give up because perseverance comes from knowing that God has called you and all your labor is unto Him. I like Jon Courson's example where he says; "Ministry is like driving a bus, people get on the bus and people get off the bus, some are going for a long ride, others only one block, but your job is to get them where they are going safely."

> *A faithful leader understands that they cannot lead others where they have not gone themselves.*

While you may never be a pastor, pastoral ministry is what every leader is called to, in other words; you become the shepherd to those God has in your life. Because people may disappoint you, it's vital to remember they are not your sheep, they're God's sheep and your job is to be a shepherd by making them the best fed, best loved sheep you can. It does not matter if you are teaching Sunday School, leading worship, or cleaning the facilities, if you have people under your care, then you are their first-line shepherd and have pastoral ministry to them. Love them with the love God has shown you because that's when you are a faithful example and a servant leader.

CHALLENGE: How do those serving with you view your leadership? Are you seen as angry with those who don't measure up? Or are you seen like Christ, always building up and offering them an example of a servant?

Chapter Seventeen

GOD CARES ABOUT YOU!

John 21:20-22 "Peter turned and saw that the disciple whom Jesus loved was following them... When Peter saw him, he asked, "Lord, what about him?" Jesus answered, "If I want him to remain alive until I return, what is that to you? You must follow me."

Jesus had a specific plan for Peter and a different plan for John. The reason God saved you is because He loves you. If you're involved in ministry it's only because God has graced you to serve Him. He doesn't need your talent, expertise or your skills. In the past God spoke through a donkey and He could do that again if needed. Although He doesn't need us, He wants us and desires fellowship with us and that's an important reminder that God wants our hearts and not just our service.

Dr. Larry Taylor says; "God is more interested in the minister than the ministry." He also says, that because He is interested in you; "Your personal fellowship with Jesus is vital." That's an important concept to remember because (especially for those in fulltime ministry), it's easy to get overwhelmed by the needs of ministry and forget that God loves you.

Your personal fellowship with Jesus is vital and that means you should spend time in prayer and the Word of God on a consistent basis. You can't receive that kind of personal fellowship when all your time with God is spent studying for or teaching others. Your personal time of devotion is for your relationship with God that you might know Him better and have fellowship with Him that's why it is vital to have your own times of prayer and devotion.

As a pastor I find that it's easy to always be studying for others, preparing for a teaching or writing an article, while I grow during those times, I find I grow more as I study for myself. The concept is that knowing God is far more important than serving Him. That's because knowing Him is the reason I exist and why I serve God.

Chuck Smith used to say; "Christianity is like the measles, you have to have it to give it away." You can never lead people closer to Christ than you are, and you can't give them what you don't have. Therefore you must be a person of prayer, a person of the Word, and a person who walks with Jesus and whose heart is fully committed to God. Remember Jesus said the greatest command is to love God with every part of

You can never lead people closer to Christ than you are, and you can't give them what you don't have.

your being, and Paul said we offer our bodies as living sacrifices in order to know the will of God *(Matthew 22:37 / Romans 12:1)*. In order to love God and offer your body back to Him, you must have a deep relationship with Him, and just like human relationships are deepened by spending time together, so your relationship with God is deeper as you spend personal, quality time with Jesus.

If you are married you must understand your first ministry is to your spouse and family, even if you're called to serve a church. The best thing you can do for your ministry is to invest in your own relationship with God, then invest in your spouse and children, finally pour into whoever God has in your life. Ron Wiseman use to say; "My ministry is to my spouse (family), my calling is to the church." That understanding has helped me to find balance when ministry needs are greater than what I can handle. My first ministry is to love my wife as Christ loved the church and gave himself for her. When I have that priority, I keep things in balance and remember; "God cares for me more than the ministry."

As you invest in your relationship with God and your relationship with your family, those are the most important investments you can ever make. Your children will remember if you spent time with them or were too busy for them. Your relationship with your spouse will go on long after the children are gone and it's sad to see husbands and wives who have little in common when their children are grown. Remember you got married for a reason, but like any relationship you must nurture your marriage and that means spending time together.

For the single person, the Apostle Paul says something very important. He tells us, the single person has more time and more freedom than those who are married, so they are to use their time wisely and be concerned about the Lord's affairs and how you can be used by God *(1 Corinthians 7:32-35)*.

Everyone who wants to be used by God must spend time in service, study, and investing in those you love. Even in recreation and having fun with your friends or family it's essential to use those times as opportunities to grow in your faith and help grow those you love. My wife, Suzanne has a wonderful ministry to our granddaughters, she is often on the phone, or having quality time with them, but always investing in teaching them how to draw near to the Lord and develop their own relationship with Christ. So, it's those with a strong relationship with God and strong personal relationships, they're the ones who making disciples and leading God's people.

> *Acts 1:8 (Jesus said) "But you will receive power when the Holy Spirit comes on you; and you will be my witnesses in Jerusalem, and in all Judea and Samaria, and to the ends of the earth."*

Those were Jesus' final words to the church before He ascended into heaven and I like to look at His words as a priority list. The Holy Spirit will give you the power to be Christ's witness, but notice where you witness. First, in Jerusalem, or your home; that speaks of those closest to you, your spouse and children, your parents or those who know you the best. Once those who really know you see you as a person of faith, then you're empowered to become a witness in Judea; IE your surrounding community. That speaks of your town, your job, your neighborhood, church, etc. Next is Samaria, or those who are hard to reach, when you've been a witness to those who know you best, and a witness to those around you, that adds credibility to your witness even to those who are hard hearted. When you live out your faith to those God has in your life, that's when you are ready to go to the ends of the earth.

When Jesus was on the mount of Transfiguration with his core team and as they came down the mountain, they were met with a man whose son was demon possessed. Jesus disciples couldn't cast the demon out of the boy but Jesus did. That's when His men asked why they couldn't cast the demon out, and Jesus said something that applies to all of life and ministry. ***Mark 9:29 NKJV ...Jesus said to them, "This kind can come out by nothing but prayer and fasting."*** It wasn't prayer and fasting right then, but a lifestyle of seeking God that would have prepared them to deal with that tough situation. So, it is for all of God's servants, it's trusting God and growing in faith every day, that's what prepares you for the toughest of times.

Tough times will come, and although you may never meet a demon possessed boy, you may face great trials in this life and if you're in ministry you will face times when things need cast out. As you recognize that God cares for you more than the work you're doing, that's when you understand that you are important to God and that's the catalyst to help you continually be growing in faith, knowledge and the wisdom of God. And that's when you're empowered for whatever God brings your way.

While holiness is a word that seems removed from our modern culture, reality is, holiness is exactly what God has for you. Your personal piety is important but you should never be viewed as being better than anyone; rather just like Jesus, you should be approachable by everyone yet unaffected by the culture or by sin. Setting boundaries in your life and understanding your personal weaknesses is essential to living a separated life. What are some of the important boundaries you might need?

First, there's the boundary of how you interface with the opposite sex. As a pastor I try not to meet with a woman by myself. If someone from the opposite sex comes into my office and needs counsel, I leave the door open and, if there's a planned counseling I have another person with me, often my wife. Just in case there are exceptions, every office in the church has a window in the door. Accountability is a simple thing and a place where many think they will never fall, but again scripture says it best;

> *1 Thessalonians 5:22 (KJV) "Abstain from all appearance of evil."*

Secondly, is the concept of being separate from the world. We are told to; "not love the world or the things of the world" *(1 John 2:15-17)*. But what does that mean?

Again, our best example is Jesus who was accused of being a "wine bibber" (I love the King James)! But Jesus was never influenced by the people of the world, rather He influenced them. Today, many in ministry seem to love the world, some of them are obvious as "prosperity teachers", but others have embraced a more subtle form of worldliness. What are those types of worldliness? There are too many to list here but examples may be found in our language, social interactions and what happens behind closed doors.

Every Christian must know their own weaknesses and areas where they can be tempted. If you have a problem with alcohol, place the boundaries in your life to keep yourself from that temptation. My personal conviction is, those in fulltime ministry should abstain from drinking any alcohol because of what it has done in our culture, *(Proverbs 31:4-7 / 1 Timothy 3:8 / Titus 2:3)* but let everyone be led by the Spirit in this area. The other big area of worldliness is in sexual behavior; far too many in the ministry have fallen in sexual compromise, in either pornography or outright fornication or adultery. Don't think you cannot fall in these areas, but remember you are flesh and have a sinful nature. It's with the Spirits power, boundaries and safeguards you can overcome. Think of the example of Joseph, who, when tempted by Potiphar's wife ran from sin instead of hanging around to fall into temptation *(Genesis 39).* Joseph had his mind set that it would be sin against God to give into her advances. Having that mindset is a boundary that will help you run away from any temptation. Remember the spirit is willing but the flesh is weak (*Matthew 26:41*) so safeguard and boundaries are critical for whatever your place of weakness is.

2 Timothy 2:22 "Flee also youthful lusts; but pursue righteousness, faith, love, (and) peace..." NKJV

Paul's advice to a young man is the same thing Joseph did, run away from the temptations that come, but Paul adds to run toward godly things, righteousness, faith, love and peace (sounds a lot like the fruit of the Spirit)!

Safeguards or personal boundaries play out in a myriad of ways for each individual but pursuing godliness is really the key. Still you must know yourself and the areas of your own temptation then place within your life safeguards to keep you from falling.

1 Peter 2:11-12 "Dear friends, I urge you, as aliens and strangers in the world, to abstain from sinful desires, which war against your soul. Live such good lives among the pagans that, though they accuse you of doing wrong, they may see your good deeds and glorify God on the day he visits us."

Peter understood the weakness of the flesh better than most. He had denied the Lord even after he boldly told Jesus; *"If everyone else abandons you, I will not!" (Matthew 26:33)* So it's Peter who fell hard that takes us to the concept of separation from the world, by living as a stranger to this world.

While the Christian life is likened to being "an alien" to the world, we are not to be so isolated we can't touch those who don't know Christ. Once again looking to Jesus for your model of holiness, He touched the lepers and hung out with sinners, yet He influenced them but they did not affect Him.

Only those who live with piety and holiness can be used by God, but piety need not mean you can't have fun or be relevant. If your personal piety gets to the place that you dress strangely or you act weirdly, you're probably not a very good witness to the world. Like Peter says;

> *"Live such a good life that even though the world accuses you of doing wrong, they will give God the glory for your good works." 1 Peter 2:12 (paraphrase mine)*

The principle is; "You are more important than the ministry." So, make sure you keep your personal relationship with Jesus fresh and make sure you keep your earthly relationships healthy. You do both of those things by always growing, always studying, never compromising, and always living by faith. Growing saints are teachable and they invest their time wisely by investing time with God and investing in those God has in their life.

The priorities of the first century church stand as an example for every generation as to how we continue to grow and be teachable. ***Acts 2:42 ...They devoted themselves to the apostles' teaching and the fellowship, to the breaking of bread and the prayers. ESV*** The early church had a devotion to the Word of God, fellowship, communion (also speaking of worship) and praying. When those disciplines are working in your life, you will continue to grow in both faith and knowledge of our Lord Jesus. As you grow you are reminded that God cares more for you than he does for the ministry you are involved in. As you remain teachable, not only will you continue to be used by God but you'll make yourself more useable because like John the Baptist you believe; ***"He must increase but I must decrease."***

CHALLENGE: Are you caring for your own soul? Do you have time for personal prayer and devotions? Do you relate to the world yet remain unaffected by the culture? Are there areas in your life that you need to repent of and ask the Holy Spirit to help you overcome? Are there places you need personal boundaries and safeguards?

CONCLUSION

I n considering the principles of ministry and faith, they are areas every Christian should take to heart. As you do – you will not only be ministering to the people God has in your life, but you will also be growing in your own faith and relationship with Jesus.

To summarize:

1. **Be Spirit Led:** It's the only way you can serve.
2. **Be a Servant:** The servant is the greatest, work for God as you rest in Christ.
3. **Don't Sweat it:** Inspiration over perspiration.
4. **Be Flexible:** The flexible will never break.
5. **God Provides:** Where God guides, He provides.
6. **Healthy things Grow:** Sheep begat sheep.
7. **Be Loyal and Submissive:** Harmony makes beautiful music.
8. **Emphasize what God has done:** Grace brings us to the heart of God.
9. **Feed God's Sheep:** The best fed and best loved sheep grow healthy.

10. **God's word has Power:** Scripture is more powerful than you know.
11. **Teach the Word:** Rightly divide the Word of Truth.
12. **Worship is Vital:** Not a show or a tune up for preaching.
13. **Be Balanced:** Avoid the extremes that divide.
14. **Prayer:** It's your lifeblood and connection to God.
15. **Know what you know:** Always fall back on the truths of God and the Bible.
16. **Be Faithful to your calling:** Love and care for those God has in your life.
17. **God cares about You:** God has a plan for you, personally (live it)!

The church should be making disciples and not just drawing people to our services. A disciple is a follower and a follower of Jesus is called to be an Ambassador of Christ. An Ambassador is one who represents someone greater than himself and represents a foreign country. So, believers are called to be strangers or aliens to the world and as we live that way, that's when we represent Jesus.

> *John 17:16 NKJV (Jesus said) "They are not of the world, just as I am not of the world."*

How you live shows you do not belong to this world and how you love shows your heart is from another world, because you follow the Master. Keeping your priorities focused is to live by faith and that is the best life you can live as you lay up treasures not here on earth, but in heaven where they will last for eternity.

It's been said; "keep the main thing the main thing" as you do, you'll not only be seen as an Ambassador for Christ, you will bear much fruit for the Lord. What's the main thing?

1 Corinthians 2:2 "For I resolved to know nothing while I was with you except Jesus Christ and him crucified."

2 Corinthians 5:21 "God made him who had no sin to be sin for us, so that in him we might become the righteousness of God."

The main thing is the Gospel and the Gospel tells us how Jesus came to bear our sin and redeem us from the empty way of life we once lived and to bring us to eternal life. The Gospel is the main thing, so be Gospel centered and those in ministry (and every believer is in the ministry) have but one message – "Jesus and Him crucified for us."

1 Corinthians 1:30 "...Jesus, who has become for us wisdom from God — that is, our righteousness, holiness and redemption."

ABOUT THE AUTHOR

P astor Rich Lammay serves as Senior Pastor of High Sierra Fellowship in Gardnerville, Nevada (a non-denominational Bible centered Church).

Pastor Rich and his wife Suzanne have been married almost 50 years; they have three grown children and eight grandchildren. They both came to faith during the 1970s Jesus Movement when God did a great work and quickly changed the Lammay's lives. Being filled with the Spirit they soon began to serve in their local church.

In 1990, along with several other families, the Lammay's helped found High Sierra Fellowship. The vision was simple, to have a church where God's Word is taught and brought into everyday life, and to facilitate worship that's exciting but free from extremes.

By January of 1992 Rich stepped into the Senior Pastor role at HSF. Two years later Pastor Rich left his high-level corporate job to pursue fulltime ministry at HSF. Since those early days Pastor Rich has earned a Bachelor of Science Degree in Biblical Studies and a Master's Degree in Theology. Both degrees are from Omega Bible Institute and Seminary (www.omega.edu).

Pastor Rich has a love for the Scriptures with his favorite book in the Bible being Galatians, and his favorite Scripture being;

Psalm 119:105 "Your word is a lamp to my feet and a light for my path".